Fire Against Fire

FIRE against FIRE

Christian Ministry
Face-to-Face with Persecution

Medardo Ernesto Gómez

Translated by Mary M. Solberg

Augsburg   Minneapolis

FIRE AGAINST FIRE
Christian Ministry Face-to-Face with Persecution

First published in Spanish as *Fuego Contra Fuego*, copyright © 1989 Medardo Ernesto Gómez.

The material by Medardo Gómez was originally presented at the Second International Conference on Hispanic Ministry, May 2–4, 1989, sponsored by Lutheran Bible Institute in California.

Scripture quotations unless otherwise noted are from the New Revised Standard Version Bible, copyright 1989, Division of Christian Education of the National Council of the Churches of Christ in the United States of America.

Cover illustrations: J. W. Smith
Cover design: Carol Evans-Smith
Map: Kim Pickering

Excerpt from Daniel Berrigan, S.J., *Steadfastness of the Saints* (Maryknoll, N.Y.: Orbis Books, 1983) on page 57 is reprinted by permission.

Excerpt from Jon Sobrino, S.J., on page 74 is reprinted with permission from *Sojourners*, Box 29272, Washington, DC 20017.

Library of Congress Cataloging-in-Publication Data
Gómez, Medardo Ernesto, 1945-
    |Fuego contra fuego.   English|
    Fire against fire : Christian ministry face-to-face with
persecution / Medardo Ernesto Gómez.
        p.   cm
    Translation of: Fuego contra fuego.
    ISBN 0-8066-2491-4 (alk. paper)
    1. Lutheran Church—El Salvador—History—20th century.
2. Persecution—El Salvador—History—20th century.   3. El Salvador—Church history—20th century.   I. Title.
BX8063.E42G65   1990
284.1'7284—dc20   90-32828
                                                                                          CIP

Manufactured in the U.S.A.   AF 9-2491

94   93   92   91   90   1   2   3   4   5   6   7   8   9   10

Contents

Translator's Preface

One of the extraordinary things about hearing the Word of God in a language other than one's native tongue is that it sounds new. It unsettles, sometimes unnerves. It requires attention, invites attentiveness, exposes points of reference previously unknown, and insists on a response. All the things hearing the Word ought somehow to do, it has a new chance to do in another language.

During the several years I lived and worked in El Salvador, I heard Scripture read in Spanish in many places and by many people. I was always astonished that somehow it seemed to have been written in that place at that time about those people, those events. God's promise of liberation; prophets' warnings; the psalmist's prayers. The tender and powerful ministry of Jesus, seeking out the left-out, confronting the established even in the imagination of their hearts. The betrayal, mockery, torture, and injustice in Jesus' passion; the cruelty of his execution. The despair of those left behind. The miracle of resurrection, the witness to new life, the hope against hope fulfilled. Paul's exhortations, thanksgivings, frustrations sounded as if they had been written then and there, in El Salvador.

On Sunday mornings at Resurrection Lutheran Church in San Salvador, Bishop Gómez always began his sermon by saying, "To gain a better understanding, let us listen again to the Word of God." Clearly and carefully, he would reread the gospel lesson, as if he wanted us to think it through with him once more before he talked about it with us. Then he would begin to preach—simply, directly, setting the context, telling the story, making the connections. And we listened to him.

Now certainly we listened because he was the preacher and it was time for the sermon. But it was more than that. There was a hunger and a thirst for the Word. And "Don Medardo," as everyone addressed him, spoke it without pretension, with the authority that came from walking with his people through the valley of the shadow of death at a time and in a place where it would have been easier to keep a low profile, speak only of the life of the world to come, and gain the favor of those in high places, instead of their suspicion.

Fire Against Fire is set against the fiery reality within which Bishop Gómez and his church have engaged in a ministry on the side of those most in need: the poor, the marginalized, the oppressed. The "theology of life" that has emerged from this ministry is itself both confession of faith and evangelization, which Bishop Gómez defines as "the communication of the love of God for humanity."

For Bishop Gómez* the experience of the Salvadoran church today is an integral part of the tradition begun by the first Christians. Their testimony, inspired by the fire of the Holy Spirit, has brought them face to face with the fire fed by the "principalities and powers" of whom Paul writes. The persecution of the Salvadoran church and its leaders has occurred because of their commitment to be in solidarity—in acts of service as well as in words of consolation—with those who suffer. This same solidarity transforms the church, inspiring its faithfulness and inciting its hope.

It has been a privilege to translate *Fire Against Fire* for English-speaking readers. I have a deep personal respect and affection for Bishop Gómez, whose witness and humanity have taught me so much during the years I have known him. His ministry has touched the lives of countless people, not only those among whom he has lived and worked on a daily basis, but among those of us who have more lately come to know and care about the church in El Salvador, the church

* The original Spanish edition was written in collaboration with Salvador Juárez.

of the poor. For our sake, even more than for theirs—for the sake of solidarity—it is important that we hear the voice of one who speaks the Word in a different language.

May it sound new. May it unsettle, perhaps unnerve. May it require attention, invite attentiveness, expose points of reference previously unknown. May it insist on a response.

—Mary M. *Solberg*
February 1990

Oscar Arnulfo Romero

You offered the bread,
The living Body
—the crushed body of your people;
its spilled blood victorious—
the peasant blood of your people
being massacred
the magical dawn will be colored
with the wine of happiness!

You knew how to drink
the double chalice
of the altar and of the people
in one single hand consecrated to service.

"Oscar Arnulfo Romero" by Monseñor Pedro Casaldáliga, translated and printed with permission.

—1

Confession of
Our Christian Principles

The New Realm of God: Proclamation of Our Lord Jesus Christ

The Christian church's primary task in any part of the world is to *evangelize*. Of course, the universal meaning of evangelization is determined by the specific cultural, social, and historical characteristics of each region. In El Salvador, as in other areas of Latin America, the word *evangelize* means to communicate the love of God according to what Scripture tells us:

> And just as Moses lifted up the serpent in the wilderness, so must the Son of Man be lifted up, that whoever believes in him may have eternal life.
>
> For God so loved the world that he gave his only Son, so that everyone who believes in him may not perish but may have eternal life. (John 3:14-16)

We understand and engage in this mission not simply because we believe in Christ. Our Christian vision and practice are based on what our Lord Jesus Christ revealed about the plans his Father, our God, has for our salvation: the Realm of Heaven. This offer of salvation is the

New Realm of God proclaimed by Jesus. It essentially has to do with life and the world as changing humanity and nature.

According to this perspective, to be Christian involves touching the individual human consciousness and the social being, as well as discovering signs of the divine in the human being, in society, and in history. In this way we strive to fulfill the gospel. We must see life from the perspective of Jesus Christ, who speaks to us about his new covenant, his liberating message based in the prophets and received from God. This is how we work to accomplish the objective that Jesus Christ set for us: to realize the foundation and new principles of his realm—*love* and *faith* that work.

Out of this spiritual experience and theological-biblical knowledge we make our Christian commitment. This is what permits us to establish an intimate and transcendent relationship between the living God and the person of flesh and blood, immersed in a real world, in a national and regional environment. Our practice, principles of ideology, and faith, as well as theology, are united with the Word of God incarnate. We believe this because we believe that in fulfilling the gospel, God chooses to identify with us, becoming like us, that is, incarnating God's own self in the people we are.

The service offered out of our evangelical, apostolic, and ecumenical vision is to build the New Realm of God; it is human, social, and spiritual action that improves society and accelerates history. Such service is commanded by God. By doing it with clarity and conviction, one lives, experiences, and observes faith; one sees, feels, and touches Christ present in each person and in each Christian community. In this way and with this spiritual content a person "puts Christ on" and "incarnates" him in daily living by bearing one's own humanity in one's struggle and one's individual and social debates, in one's work for the good news, which is undertaken and transcended by love.

Calling, profession, talent, and ministry are offered with humility and strength from God, principally with concern for the needy, the most impoverished, those who suffer most in natural and humanly made misfortunes. These are our brothers and sisters, who are the victims of earthquakes, floods, war, and of unjust and oppressive social orders.

The Mission of Our Church

The mission of our church is to proclaim the love of God—the love that God delivered for salvation, as a testimony and guarantee of the New Realm: God's own beloved, God's only Son, the chosen one, Jesus Christ our Lord.

Christ is our Savior, because he came to show us this path, this truth, this way of being, of living, of transcending the levels of human consciousness, to the point of being able to perceive that I AM of our own, that I AM of each one, "our daily Yahweh" [as in our daily bread]. This is in accordance with the active gospel of life and history. It is in this prophetic dimension that we feel we are acting consistently with the way Jesus evangelized. We follow after him in his ministry. For this reason we feel we also are faithful servants with the Word of God our Father, who said through the apostles: "This is my Son, my Chosen; listen to Him!" (Luke 9:35)

Christ's Project of Salvation and His Resurrection

Jesus provided us with a new plan of salvation, the Realm of God, that is, the Realm of Life, which is opposed to death. Here the *theology of life* is born, which begins out of the dynamic interaction among the human being, the life of nature, and social-historical conditions.

This theology is unique, universal, and transformative. It has to do with God's interest and presence in life. Based on what Jesus taught us, diverse ways of reflecting on the Word of God can be derived from this theology. But the center must always be life, just as the center of our church and social work is Jesus Christ our Lord.

If God is the I AM, that is, Being, the vital principle, life itself; if God is the Word, the knowledge, the energy, and the voice of the consciousness; if God is the most profound transformative force of the human being and the universe, then it is this theology's obligation to be the defender and promoter of life, of the sacred rights of human beings, of society, and of nature—because where there is life, there is God. To reflect on the Word of God means to relate it, carry it, or make it spring forth from life and from the historical moment in which we live. The Realm of God is equivalent to the Realm of Life. So in order to build it we must follow Christ in humanizing time and space by doing what Jesus taught us to do.

Life is light, liberation, justice, well-being, peace, and love. If these do not exist, there may be existence but not life in God's eyes nor in Christ's presence. For it is Christ who, incarnated in our suffering people, proclaims that life, that New Realm of God. In order to promote this realm we must proclaim the Word and work with love in service to others. This means sharing the good news with the poor, and condemning and confronting sin.

The Resurrection: Fire that Conquers Fire

Jesus came and conquered death for all time with the fire that he brought to earth (Luke 12:49-51). He rescues life with his resurrection; hope is born again dressed anew in his spirit, and faith is awakened. Our God is a conqueror, the God of life—and of life in abundance! But Jesus Christ our Lord had to unite his fire with the fire of the human heart, the fire of history in order to gain the victory that led to his glorification. His fire as God's chosen one had to burn against the fire of evil.

Jesus could not avoid confronting the fire, the fire of the cross. This was personified through his passion in torture, betrayal, incomprehension, threats of death, and false accusations. The fire of the cross was revealed in various tests Jesus had to experience as a human being. His own faith as the Son of God would emerge out of the fire of the cross. The thought and the example of Peter emerged from this same conviction, when he speaks to us of faith in the face of different tests: "The genuineness of your faith—being more precious than gold that, though perishable, is tested by fire—may be found to result in praise and glory and honor when Jesus Christ is revealed" (1 Peter 1:7).

At the hour of his resurrection Jesus reveals himself to us transformed into eternal life with all the fervor and intensity of the Holy Spirit. This is why the resurrection is the victory of the fire that conquers fire in the real, human, and historical life of Jesus, as in the life of all who believe in the gospel.

This spiritual force alone, this fire, has kept the testimony of the resurrected one alive. Jesus lives in each baptized person and in everyone who believes in him. Throughout the world, whatever circumstances or human and social conditions a believer lives in, there is Jesus. The Holy Spirit through prayer and action inspires and guides us toward the realization that God's realm is manifested everywhere.

Jesus is found wherever there is a believer: in the street, in the home, the factory, workshops, schools, offices, refugee camps, hospitals, jails, garrisons, battle zones, in the mountains, and in the city. God is present with the true disciple, struggling against oppression, misery, captivity, and death.

The Divine Fire and the Fire of Evil

In this essay I will distinguish between two concepts of *fire*: First, the divine fire of God, the fire of life; second, the fire of evil, of death, of sin, of Satan. These two fires struggle with one another in the life, passion, and death of Jesus Christ, until the fire of life, God, prevails through the resurrection.

From that time on, among the first Christians and all future generations of believers, the Holy Spirit is identified as a latent fire, constant energy, perennial activity, fuel that moves human beings, a "foundry fire" in the heart "like a burning fire" that is not extinguished. This spirit generates the forward movement of history, the thought and the works of epochs and civilizations. This same "burning fire" purifies the conscience. This spirit, this fire, this energy, this I AM, this heightened level of vitality, is God, who also acts like a purifying fire. "Who can endure the day of his coming, and who can stand when he appears? For he is like a refiner's fire and like fullers' soap" (Mal. 3:2).

The divine fire of life, the Holy Spirit, impels us, sustains us, and gives us courage to work good. Faith, a spiritual strength, emerges in the intrepid and audacious actions of heroes, martyrs, prophets, apostles, and all the servants of the Lord.

The divine fire confronts the fire of hell, which tries to prevent the construction of the New Realm, and fervently tries to exercise and maintain the dominion of evil. Our Savior Jesus Christ was the first one who confronted this fire. His first test is recounted in the story of the temptations in the desert. The devil, with malicious intelligence, tries to persuade Jesus by using God's own words. Jesus struggles to conquer the evil spirit, the voice of Satan. He burns the temptations "with unquenchable fire" (Luke 3:17).

Here the Holy Spirit revives our Lord with the divine Word's purifying fire. The demon, burning with the fire of evil, attacks Jesus by offering power and riches and quotes from Scripture in order to tempt him to fall into sin. The temptations were aimed to obstruct the ministry of the Son of God. Jesus speaks to the demon with the voice of his Father: "Away with you, Satan! for it is written, 'Worship the Lord your God, and serve only him'" (Matt. 4:10). Jesus sets the fire of God against the fire of the demon. In the final temptation he rebukes the demon: Listen, spirit of evil, "It is said, 'Do not put the Lord your God to the test'" (Luke 4:12).

Having emerged from this first test, Jesus is ready to begin his ministry—a ministry of the fire of life against the fire of death.

Encounter in the Ministry of Jesus Christ: Fire Against Fire

It is with love and faith that Jesus faces the people and circumstances that determine his whole life. St. Mark tells us that a leper, on his knees, presents himself before Jesus and says, "If you choose, you can make me clean." Jesus has mercy, cures him, and commands him not to tell anyone. But the leper divulges the secret and begins to tell everyone. Because of this Jesus can no longer freely enter the city (Mark 1:40-45).

As I interpret this story in the context of El Salvador, I am sure that Jesus knew that this first miracle would create problems. He knew that it would be misunderstood, that a battle between the fire of perdition and the fire of salvation would soon begin. It was for this same reason—for security—that Jesus advises the leper, "See that you say nothing to anyone." But the love of God cannot help doing good, whatever the opposition.

Despite Jesus' request, the uproar created by the leper's news is not created in bad faith. When the leper is healed, his thanks to the Lord overflows; he cannot keep silent. He tells the story throughout the region. As a result, Jesus can no longer enter the city of Jerusalem, which

24

will later become a place of torture for him. This is why his disciples advise him not to go.

Jerusalem already signified death. John the Baptist, the herald of Christ, was condemned to death when he denounced the false spirituality of the scribes and Pharisees, and the imperial corruption. This event reveals the destiny of whoever dares to fulfill God's mission. Nonetheless Jesus Christ did so by becoming the Suffering Servant. The conditions of oppression that filled his life were the same as those his people suffered. By denouncing injustice he invited the sword, the whip, the nails, and the cross.

—2

The Historical Place of Our Ministry

The First Christians

If Jesus had not been the Son of God, the hoped-for Messiah, everything would have ended with his crucifixion and death. Christ arose just as the Scriptures prophesied. For his followers, disciples, and apostles, whose witness is recorded in the New Testament, Christ's resurrection became the spiritual foundation, the basis of the faith, so that "the Son of man [must] be lifted up" (John 3:14) throughout time, incarnate in the people in his movement through history.

The divine revelation that Christ communicates by his resurrection occurs when his followers are hungry and thirsty for faith. They are experiencing moments of tribulation after the trial, sentence, and death of their pastor and prophet. How will they continue Christ's ministry? Jesus' resurrection and appearances to his followers not only sustain the individual's faith but transcend to the Christian community.

The fire of the new covenant is born with the resurrection of Christ. The Holy Spirit fills Christians, who now have the spiritual power to defend themselves against the challenges of evil. The letter to the Ephesians tells how the first Christian communities strengthened their faith:

Finally, be strong in the Lord and in the strength of his power. Put on the whole armor of God, so that you may be able to stand against the wiles of the devil. For our struggle is not against enemies of blood and flesh, but against the rulers, against the authorities, against the cosmic powers of this present darkness, against the spiritual forces of evil in the heavenly places. Therefore take up the whole armor of God, so that you may be able to withstand on that evil day, and having done everything, to stand firm. Stand therefore, and fasten the belt of truth around your waist, and put on the breastplate of righteousness. As shoes for your feet put on whatever will make you ready to proclaim the gospel of peace. With all of these, take the shield of faith, with which you will be able to quench all the flaming arrows of the evil one. Take the helmet of salvation, and the sword of the Spirit, which is the word of God.

Pray in the Spirit at all times in every prayer and supplication. To that end keep alert and always persevere in supplication for all the saints. Pray also for me, so that when I speak, a message may be given to me to make known with boldness the mystery of the gospel, for which I am an ambassador in chains. Pray that I may declare it boldly, as I must speak. (Eph. 6:10-20)

This is how the disciples and first Christian communities endured the persecution they suffered for preaching the gospel. The freedom that

Christ gave them—and exercising that freedom, in not recognizing Caesar as king—cost them a great deal. They were persecuted by those who wanted to erase the name of Christ. This same freedom was the fire for their defense—for acting, speaking, and baptizing in the name of the Father and of the Son and of the Holy Spirit.

History recalls the testimony of martyrs who, faithful to the name of Christ, prevailed over evil and over those who desired to eliminate his name from the planet. In the end the persecutors were ashamed of their evil and were convinced that God was with the Christians, just as on Calvary, Jesus' captors and executioners recognized that Jesus Christ was the Son of man: ''. . . 'Certainly this man was innocent.' And when all the crowds who had gathered there for this spectacle saw what had taken place, they returned home, beating their breasts'' (Luke 23:47-48).

One of the great testimonies of Christ's love was the conversion worked in the persecutors of the first Christians. St. Paul was transformed from a persecutor into a servant of the Lord—''an apostle of Christ Jesus by the will of God''—a sower of the faith, foolish for the cross, and an inexhaustible worker for Christ Jesus our Lord,

> . . . because he judged me faithful and appointed me to his service, even though I was formerly a

31

blasphemer, a persecutor, and a man of violence. But I received mercy because I had acted ignorantly in unbelief.... The saying is sure and worthy of full acceptance, that Christ Jesus came into the world to save sinners—of whom I am the foremost. But for that very reason I received mercy, so that in me, as the foremost, Jesus Christ might display the utmost patience, making me an example to those who would come to believe in him for eternal life. (1 Tim. 1:12-13, 15-16)

The Fire of God in the First Christians

The Book of Acts records that the pioneers of Christianity lived through great danger and took unforeseen risks. Nonetheless, the protective fire never failed them. In keeping with the promise that our Lord Jesus Christ had made, when the first believers were taken before the authorities, God gave them the words and wisdom necessary to respond in their interrogations. This converted moments of danger into occasions for giving testimony:

See, I am sending you out like sheep into the midst of wolves; so be wise as serpents and innocent as doves. Beware of them, for they will hand you over to councils and flog you in their synagogues; and you will be dragged before governors and kings because of me, as a testimony to them and the Gentiles. When they hand you over, do not worry about how you are to speak or what you are to say; for what you are to say will be given to you at that time; for it is not you who speak, but the Spirit of your Father speaking through you. (Matt. 10:16-20)

The fire of the Holy Spirit was poured out on the first disciples on Pentecost (Acts 2:1-20). They spread this fire through prayer and the unity of faith by their acts and preaching. The Book of Acts tells us how the fire of Christ began to disseminate after the apostles had been filled with the Holy Spirit at Pentecost. This is how the first community of Christians expanded:

So those who welcomed his message were baptized, and that day about three thousand persons were added. They devoted themselves to the apostles' teaching and fellowship, to the breaking of bread and the prayers. . . .

All who believed were together and had all things in common; they would sell their possessions and goods and distribute the proceeds to all, as any had need. Day by day, as they spent much time together in the temple, they broke bread at home and ate their food with glad and generous hearts, praising God and having the

goodwill of all the people. And day by day the
Lord added to their number those who were
being saved. (Acts 2:41-47)

Source of Faith and Example of
Love and Service

The Book of Acts contains a treasure of testimonies for Christians of all generations. It is one
of the inexhaustible sources of the faith, of in-
spiration for church and pastoral work, one of
the classics of the Bible. In it we find both the
anguish of that historical period and the excite-
ment of the collective efforts of the early church.
We see not only the example of Christian heroes
and martyrs, but also the epic of their apostolate,
practice, ideology, and christology. There is a living relationship between their painstaking work
to spread the gospel and the organizing of the
early congregations.

The first Christian communities were called
together through love as service. The Book of Acts
illustrates this spirit of social action. It also provides a realistic account of the martyrdom of that
period, the anguish Christians suffered. They suffered persecution, prison, and the punishment of
death because they were loyal to the name of
Christ Jesus. Many were stoned, burned alive,

crucified right side up and upside down. St. Peter died on a cross with his feet toward heaven. That part of Christianity's history reveals the high cost of discipleship. It helps us remember those condemned to forced labor, to the dungeons, to the whip, and to the clutches of wild animals, simply because they were believers in the gospel and had faith in Christ Jesus our Lord.

St. Paul describes other forms of suffering he and other apostles underwent: hunger, thirst, nakedness, assault, homelessness, exhaustion, and curses. We suffer persecution and we endure it, he says—and even then they defame us. We have come to be scorned by all.

The apostles and the first Christians, baptized and filled with the Holy Spirit, received that divine fire, that power of the Spirit. This made possible their ministry of fire against the fire of evil, so that the fire of Christ might reach and embrace more hearts.

The Promise of the Church in the World

Just as Jesus had announced, the earth—beginning with the first Christians—begins to burn, immediately after his resurrection and glorification. The fire of God spreads into the world through each believer, through each community that is receptive to the good news, which is communicated by the servants of the gospel. As Jesus had said: "I came to bring fire to the earth, and how I wish it were already kindled! I have a baptism with which to be baptized, and what stress I am under until it is completed!" (Luke 12:49-50)

God poured out the Spirit over the apostles just as at Pentecost. Now the divine fire, the fire of Christ, is poured out burning over the whole world, beginning with his disciples, his followers, and the first communities. With humility, intelligence, and gaining courage from the strategies the Word of God inspires in them, these proclaimers carry the good news to the poor, just as God directs them.

During Jesus' ministry he helped his followers understand to whom the good news was directed: "At that time Jesus said, 'I thank you, Father, Lord of heaven and earth, because you have hidden these things from the wise and the intelligent and have revealed them to infants; yes, Father, for such was your gracious will'" (Matt. 11:25-26). It was with simplicity that Christ Jesus preached his message to those he had chosen.

Later the apostle Paul tells us:

Contribute to the needs of the saints; extend hospitality to strangers.

Bless those who persecute you; bless and do not curse them. . . . Live in harmony with one another; do not be haughty, but associate with the lowly; do not claim to be wiser than you are. (Rom. 12:13-14, 16)

Therefore we ourselves boast of you among the churches of God for your steadfastness and faith during all your persecutions and the afflictions that you are enduring. (2 Thess. 1:4)

The first Christians continued the evangelizing mission of Jesus Christ in this way: "Listen, my beloved brothers and sisters. Has not God chosen the poor in the world to be rich in faith and to be heirs of the kingdom that he has promised to those who love him?" (James 2:5)

Later the author of Revelation envisioned the promise of the church in the world:

Then I heard a loud voice in heaven, proclaiming, "Now have come the salvation and the power and the kingdom of our God and the authority of his Messiah, for the accuser of our comrades has been thrown down, who accuses them day and night before our God.

"But they have conquered him by the blood of the Lamb and by the word of their testimony, for they did not cling to life even in the face of death. Rejoice then, you heavens and those who dwell in them!

"But woe to the earth and the sea, for the devil has come down to you with great wrath, because he knows that his time is short!" (Rev. 12:10-12)

———3

The Fire of Christ's Ministry in El Salvador's Present Moment

A Confession of the Reality and the Faith of the Lutheran Church in El Salvador

As pastor, evangelist, and bishop of our Salvadoran Lutheran church, I see our people believing and taking part in the divine project. As part of the body of Christ we are experiencing today situations similar to those the first Christians faced in developing their ministry.

The first Christians are our model of the gift for ministry. In fervent devotion to the Christian cause, faithful to the name of the Lord, they struggled against all kinds of oppression. With the help of the divine fire, the protective fire of the Holy Spirit, they struggled against that which sought to bind the freedom of the Word of our Lord Jesus Christ, which proclaimed the good news to the poor: the New Realm of God. The first Christian communities are a spiritual model for our communities in El Salvador. The dynamics of their faith and the historical dimensions of their concerns are very much alike.

What was Jerusalem when Jesus arrived? Historians say it was like a forgotten corner of the world, a place of misery, slavery, plagues, and sicknesses. There was corruption at all levels, from the dominant powers to individuals submerged in prostitution, vice, false laws, and meaningless customs. Nevertheless, the Son of man came to that place and was incarnated in those who suffered poverty, exploitation, and sin. He was living proof that God never forgets God's own.

Just what is the historical framework within which we are developing our Christian ministry in El Salvador today? Our social, political, historical, and economic conditions could be summarized as extreme poverty, constant violations of fundamental human rights, the rule of corruption, crime, vice, and "false consciousness." All of this is the outcome of a history filled with economic and social inequalities that have deepened to the point of misery. Violence and terror happen daily throughout our country.

The war within our borders, among our own, has enormous costs to our people. As the crisis deepens, polarization provokes greater confrontation among brothers and sisters, between popular groups and the security forces of the government—among the poor themselves. The city and the countryside are sitting on a powder keg. We are living between two major belligerent forces; some fight for peace, social justice, and well-being; others, who do not want the oppressed to be free, promote and intensify the war.

A large proportion of the poor majority of our population lives in very difficult conditions as a result of the political-military crisis and natural disasters. Many live in refugee camps, in exile, in marginal areas around the large cities, or "repopulations" [rural communities formed by refugees who have decided to leave refugee camps in San Salvador, or have decided to return from camps in neighboring Honduras, to try to make a new start near their places of origin].

The situation in El Salvador is made more complex by the fact that we are bound up in the conflict that engulfs all of Central America. Something is occurring that is similar to what happened when Jesus entered Jerusalem. The church must play the role that Jesus Christ assumed, demonstrating that God has not forgotten the world. The church must show that, on the contrary, God loves the world. That is why God is incarnate in the world, to be part of the world, getting to know and serving it. The gospel is incarnated in this Christian plan.

The Call to Our Church

A time came when the Lord called us as a church to give greater testimony of praise and service.

God gave us the opportunity to fulfill the mission of evangelization, communicating the love of God in a way that would relate to the preaching of life and history. What did God propose during the 1970s, when a social and pastoral hope arose in the heart of our church, just as the present armed conflict was gathering strength?

The first elements of God's proposal are the "permanent elements" handed down to us by the followers of the Lord and the original Christian communities. As a church we have to commit ourselves to "contribute, in the name of God, to favor those most in need, committing ourselves at the same time to work toward the solution of national and international problems, for the construction of the Realm of God." These two postulates clearly state what a tremendous responsibility we have as a church.

When we found ourselves faced with the task of carrying out the practice of Christian ministry in these conditions, we thought: How can we do it in an atmosphere that appears to be governed by evil and promotes sin? Following through on our commitment made us afraid. We wanted to escape, to evade that commitment. But our Lord Jesus Christ took us with all his strength and, in spite of everything including our fear, has sustained us to serve him.

I want to tell you about this fire that makes us so afraid, that tortures and sickens us. But I will also testify about the other fire, the fire of divine warmth that makes it possible for the church to continue.

The Fire of Christ in the Faith and Action of Our Church

What did we confront during our pastoral and social ministry, given the conditions of our country? We must refer to the letter to the Ephesians to respond to this question:

> Put on the whole armor of God, so that you may be able to stand against the wiles of the devil. For our struggle is not against enemies of blood and flesh, but against the rulers, against the authorities, against the cosmic powers of this present darkness, against the spiritual forces of evil in the heavenly places. (Eph. 6:11-12)

The symbols and identities that incarnate evil in our world actually exist, are actively present, and are using their fire power to attack the work of God.

There are modern tyrannical powers that set themselves against the liberation of the people of God. There are various Caesars that want to be adored, to be recognized as God. Today, as in the days of the first Christians, there are centurions, Pharisees, jail keepers, Pilates, and executioners, who remain ready to oppress those who cry out for justice, respect, and a life of dignity.

To be pastors or believers in these conditions means to be accused of being political, subversive, communist. It means to orient the people, to be spiritual guides, social workers, and friendly counselors. It also means being prophetic, pointing out individual and social sin, and helping the people interpret the signs of God. Proclaiming the good news to the poor here means to be ready to be martyred, martyred in the sense of being a witness with one's work and life. To be a servant of God is to give testimony to life.

Developing our ministry in such circumstances has produced spiritual growth in us. We are thankful to the call of Christ Jesus by the will of God, and thankful for this marvelous opportunity to serve our neighbors in the name of the gospel.

What we have accomplished spiritually we see reflected in religious activities. Our worship services and other aspects of faith have daily significance. The cross no longer symbolizes submission or masochistic suffering; it has been converted into the experience of profound love. Prayer is no longer a mere religious custom, but a necessity inherent in life.

What have we as a church done in the face of persecution, attacks, captures, and death threats? What have we done out of our Christian ethic? I would like to quote a brief passage from an advertisement published by the Salvadoran Lutheran Synod following the criminal and sacrilegious bombing of the Lutheran Church of the Resurrection in San Salvador on December 28, 1988, as evidence of the spiritual growth we have experienced under such conditions.

Christian faith serves in these cases to add to our commitment. In the face of the most recent attack we have met to reflect and meditate together, inspired by the Bible and with the spiritual strength given us by the testimony of Jesus Christ. In these moments, with the illuminating Word of God and the sanctifying presence of the Holy Spirit, we have prayed for those who, driven by evil, work against our Christian church, asking for their repentance, pardon, and conversion. Prayer and reflection about our faith have been our responses to the hate poured out against the church. These are the two spiritual paths we have encouraged our church and our communities to follow.... ("Faith is our concrete work"—Lutheran Synod of El Salvador—published in *La Prensa Gráfica* and *El Diario de Hoy*, daily newspapers of San Salvador, January 7, 1989.)

Other activities that have expressed heightened levels of spirituality occur as we have accompanied, comforted, and been in solidarity with refugees, victims of the earthquake, and those who have returned from refugee camps abroad to their homes in El Salvador. We have lived through these exoduses. We have been with our brothers and sisters from the start of their repopulation efforts and in the construction of their new communities.

On several occasions we have accompanied brothers and sisters who have been repatriated from the refugee camps in Honduras to their homes in El Salvador. When serious difficulties have beset these caravans—when moments of tension, confrontation, and danger have occurred—our faith has been strongest. On the road at the border crossing, the fire of prayer was ignited as we linked our hands and hearts to request God's presence.

The church is nourished by injustice, pain, and suffering. It feels united with the poor, because it is from the poor that this spirituality is received. Not only do they give us hope; they also teach us. . . . In this way God can clear up many doubts, reaching into what is hidden to become manifest as a more human God, a God who lives with us and is raised up in our longings and hopes. A God who does not speak in philosophies or difficult reflections, nor in lofty speculations, but rather as our people speak—with a *guanaco* [colloquial term for Salvadoran] accent.

The Love of God Expressed in Service

When we heard the Lord's call through the cry of our poor and suffering people, we decided to respond like Jesus. In our work and service we have experienced moments of weakness, virtually renouncing the cause. However, we have also had times of great courage, satisfaction, joy, and happiness. Our pastoral and social life has unfolded between these two poles.

In the name of God we have succeeded in our service. During the early 1980s we were able to save the lives of some brothers and sisters who were fleeing death. We moved them from areas of conflict to the refuge "Faith and Hope." Although not all their needs were met, at least they were safe. They were grateful for this Christian help. Nevertheless, we advised them not to tell anyone, to avoid speculations and misunderstandings. But they were so grateful that they went and spread the news everywhere, with the result that suspicions began to arise against us. From then on the accusations, persecution, imprisonment, deaths, threats, and attacks against us intensified.

These brothers and sisters, along with others who had been displaced from their homes, formed the new community of Panchimilama [a repopulation formed primarily by inhabitants of "Faith and Hope" refugee community]. Both Panchimilama and the Christian mission "Faith and Hope" have been attacked with dynamite by evil forces that want to extinguish the fire of the love of God with all the fire of their hate.

This sinful reaction to our Christian work is due to the misunderstanding and bad faith of those who have judged us and treated us with prejudice and the fire of destruction. In the cause of the poor, it seems that the church is not permitted to participate in the things of this world.

We are singled out because we see our ministry as synonymous with evangelization. Our aim is to communicate the love of God to the oppressed, those who are in prison, in refugee camps, in the repopulations, those whose hearts are broken, those who ask for help in understanding difficult aspects of their own lives, the lives of their families, and the life of their nation. Those who misinterpret what we do accuse us and oppose our humanitarian, Christian work.

But we cannot stop identifying ourselves with those who are in greatest need. We see their sad and desolate faces in the refugee camps, the repopulation sites, and the new communities built with the pain, sacrifice, and hope of the displaced. Most of these people are without jobs, without documents, and fearful for their own security. They feel more broken having lost their families and belongings because of the violence.

It has not been easy to speak of the love of God to those who are dying of hunger and lack the other basic necessities of life. This is why we feel a compelling urgency to evangelize not only by speaking, by saying "God loves you," but also with actions that demonstrate God's love. We must fulfill this mission even if it means risking our lives, offering them in adoration of God and in service to our neighbors.

Personal Experience

The early 1980s were years of horrendous crimes. The war began to intensify; the struggle of those groups that had taken up arms widened, under-written by greater military strength. The army and security forces of El Salvador's government responded. Desperately seeking their enemies, the government confused them with anyone who spoke up for justice, peace, and well-being. As the war mentality intensified so did injustice and the fire of death. Terrorist groups on the right also emerged; they blindly justified political assassinations by saying they were fighting against communism.

My own situation indicates this repression: I was kidnapped by one of these death squads, which accused me of being a subversive and threatened to murder me. But God did not allow that to happen. God saved me and converted me into a servant, prepared to testify to his love by proclaiming God's salvation, which through life, Word, and works declares the love of God.

I want to help orient our church with this commitment by issuing a clear call: "Those who lose their life for [Jesus'] sake will find it" (Matt. 16:25). In the face of misinterpretations, we now know that these are the risks we run as Christians, even when the truth speaks for itself.

This experience has made it crystal clear that "the Church cannot coexist with political interests determined by any particular group, for to do so would be to corrupt the essence of the nature of the Christian. It would be to submit faith and love to schemes elaborated coldly, schemes that mutilate the creativity and the spontaneity of Christian truth and practice."

It is with this thinking that we have developed our ministry. Since its inception it has created an extraordinary phenomenon within our entire community: the Salvadoran Lutheran church has become news in every corner of El Salvador. Those who suffer began to identify themselves with our church.

We have carried out our ministry in the name of God. But along with spiritual growth, our pastoral and social activities have called forth the powerful opposition of evil. Church families are taken prisoner, become refugees, and go into exile.

Courageous members of our communities have been murdered. People like Rev. David Fernández, a martyr of our church, have sacrificed their lives struggling with the fire of the gospel. David was kidnapped and murdered by members of El Salvador's armed forces. His body was pulled from a ditch near the city of San Miguel on November 21, 1984.

In his last sermon to the Lutheran community in San Miguel, David Fernández responded to the great fear he sensed among his people. He told them: "Without God, we are defenseless.

With God we are secure." Our martyred pastor David Fernández has joined the history of brothers and sisters who have had to struggle, battling fire with fire, because they were witnesses for Christ. Our brother and pastor is part of the history of martyrdom and religious persecution in El Salvador. His living example helps illuminate the path of evangelization we must follow.

The Gospel and Our History

During these times biblical history is our teacher. The life and the experience of our people is also a source of biblical and theological reflection. Much of the Bible, especially the Gospels, can only be understood through the experience of suffering. Those moments from which Christianity emerged are relived in the experience of suffering. In El Salvador, the best source for Christian reflection is historical reality.

The Bible describes times when the fire of evil appears to be winning. For example, the apostles and first Christians are downcast at the death of their pastor and prophet Jesus Christ. It seems that fear and panic, discouragement and failure, prevail among the faithful.

I wish to close with the biblical message that gives all of us security in the face of downheartedness; that is the historical, hope-inspiring account of the resurrection. There is no human grief that will not be transformed in the future glory. The divine fire is the fire of the gospel, which will devour the forces of evil. ". . . [T]hrough faith [they] quenched raging fire, escaped the edge of the sword, won strength out of weakness, became mighty in war, put foreign armies to flight" (Heb. 11:34).

Medardo Gómez and
the Church's Struggle in El Salvador

Let us attempt to define the pastor's crime; it bears uncommon interest for us also.

It is this: he dares lead the common life of Christians. He opens his Bible; he reads there certain instructions and commendations. And then he proceeds to act, in the breach as he is, to act in the manner in which Christians throughout history have acted. He breaks through the smog of pseudonormalcy; he speaks out against unjust laws; he objects to murder. And worse still, he invites others to do likewise.

No wonder he is in trouble! For he exhibits openly before the world those characteristics extolled in his tradition and defamed by the state: courage, imagination, tenacity, solidarity with others.

> —*Daniel Berrigan, S.J., after*
> *meeting Medardo Gómez in San*
> *Salvador in 1983 (from*
> Steadfastness of the Saints)

St. Peter's Catholic Church in Washington, D.C., was filled to overflowing on the morning of January 23, 1990. Church leaders from throughout the U.S. had come to stand in solidarity with the churches of El Salvador. I, along with 15 other missionaries to El Salvador present that day, had been forced to leave our adopted country in the previous weeks, whether by threats, or by deportation, or simply because there was no longer any space to do the work we had been sent to do. All of us hoped to return in coming months.

The special guests from that beautiful but anguished land called "The Savior" were Rev. Edgar Palacios, an exiled Baptist minister; Father Octavio Cruz, former head of the social service work of the Archdiocese of San Salvador; Lucy, a representative of the Catholic Base Christian Communities; and Medardo Gómez, bishop of the Salvadoran Lutheran Synod.

Jorge Lara-Braud, a theologian from San Francisco who had been a personal friend of the martyred Salvadoran Archbishop Oscar Romero, made some introductory comments to Bishop Gómez' talk. He declared unequivocally, "Medardo Gómez is the heir to the mantle of Oscar Romero." When it came time for Gómez to speak, he was greeted by a lengthy standing ovation.

Who is this man, who just a few years ago was virtually unknown outside of his own tiny church, but whose name is now mentioned in the same breath as that of Oscar Romero, Saint of the Americas?

Contrasting and seemingly contradictory images abound in the person of Medardo Ernesto Gomez, bishop of the Lutheran Synod of El Salvador:

—After being consecrated by a Swedish Lutheran bishop under apostolic succession, wearing full liturgical vestments, the new bishop processes down the aisle under a canopy of cornstalks lovingly prepared by the peasant farmers who transformed their austere refugee camp into an open-air cathedral the day before. Journalists have called Gómez the "Bishop of the Refugees."

—In black suit and clergy collar, Medardo Gómez poses for a photo alongside Costa Rican president Oscar Arias in Oslo, Norway. Gómez was invited as a special guest by the Norwegian government for the presentation to Arias of the Nobel prize.

—Donning a baseball cap to shield the hot noonday sun, and wearing sneakers to better traverse the thick dust and slippery gravel, a slightly overweight bishop accompanies his fellow Lutherans from the city, down the steep hill, to the refugee community of Panchimilama. Later in the day, during a simple but lively liturgy accompanied by guitars and violins, he steps into the communion line along with all the others present, to receive the bread and wine from a lay catechist, a 45-year-old peasant woman who had recently survived the massacre of 50 people in her community. She and her family had subsequently found refuge with the Lutheran church.

—In one more of a seemingly endless succession of Saturday night dinner meetings with visiting church delegations at the Gómez home, guests are graciously treated to a traditional Salvadoran meal, a moving presentation by the bishop and his wife Abelina, and folk dances by the Gómez children. "You are a great gift to us," he tells the humbled group of gringos. "Your solidarity has kept us alive."

—As thousands of members of the Catholic, Episcopal, Baptist, and Lutheran churches, along with peasants, trade unionists, women's groups, and students take to the streets of San Salvador in a "March for Peace," Medardo Gómez leads the way with pastors and members of the more than 20 Lutheran congregations. The children wave palm branches adorned with brightly colored flowers. In spite of unrelenting repression against churches that actively work for peace with justice, the Lutheran church continues to grow, but it has become almost completely a "church of the poor."

—It's the last night of a three-day pastors' retreat. Our pastors have been maligned by many for their lack of formal education. Some of their communities have been threatened by the army for being involved with a "subversive" church. They are tired and a bit afraid, given the bewildering flow of events adversely affecting their communities. Bishop Gómez spends several hours talking with them, listening to their problems, and encouraging them to take steps forward with their communities. Pastor of pastors—this is Medardo Gómez at his best.

When I began my work with the Lutheran Synod of El Salvador in 1986, I felt very strongly that this church would not survive if Gómez were to be exiled or killed. Three and a half years later, this ragtag group of pastors is carrying on the work of the Lutheran church in El Salvador, while their bishop has become a refugee. A fellow missionary still in El Salvador has described the work of the pastors and their congregations as "heroic." The gradual building up of the grassroots congregational base of the Salvadoran Lutheran church has happened quietly, little known to church people outside the country.

These images, among many others, are the essence of Medardo Gómez for me. To know the man, you need to walk with him. This compact book gives a glimpse of the man and his church. It is filled with the concepts that guide Gómez' ministry—the Theology of Life, an emphasis on prayer followed by action, the special attention given to the most needy, a profound understanding of the priesthood of all believers, and more. But to really know the man, you would need to see him ministering among the poor of El Salvador, the people he most enjoys and loves.

Medardo Gómez doesn't talk much about his own life. He has said many times that until he was converted by the poor, there was not much in his life that would be of special interest to others. He led a simple, relatively uneventful life until the refugees came to the steps of the Lutheran church in 1982.

Medardo was born in San Miguel, El Salvador, on June 8, 1945. His father, Juan Gilberto Gómez, was an industrial mechanic. His mother, Rosenda Gómez, taught grade school. From an early age, young Medardo wanted to be a priest. He was refused entrance to the seminary because his parents, like the majority of Salvadorans, were not married in the church.

At the invitation of David Fernández (who later became a Lutheran pastor and was assassinated in 1984), Medardo Gómez joined the Lutheran church in 1964. In 1966 he went to Augsburg Lutheran Seminary in Mexico City, where he graduated in 1970. He also received a Master's in Education at the Francisco Gavidia University of San Salvador in 1982. On August 6, 1986, he was consecrated the first bishop of the Salvadoran Lutheran Synod. While at the seminary in Mexico, Gómez met his wife to be, Abelina Centeno. They have six children.

Bishop Gómez has received numerous international awards, including an honorary doctorate from Trinity Lutheran Seminary, Columbus, Ohio, in 1985, the Confessor of Christ Award from the Lutheran School of Theology at Chicago in 1988. He will receive the David W. Preus Leadership Award from Luther Northwestern Theological Seminary, St. Paul, Minnesota, in 1990.

Medardo Gómez has been called a subversive, sometimes a communist, by people in his country and ours, by people both in and outside the church. But these labels put Gómez in good company. It's the same thing they said about Archbishop Romero; the same thing they said about the countless Christians who have been killed in the name of national security in El Salvador. But when you meet the man, when you see him ministering among his people, the labels melt away and you see a man who takes his Christian faith seriously. A man who above all else wants to follow Christ. He doesn't want to be a hero. He is often afraid, especially for his family. But he sees a sinful situation within his country; he names it and calls people to conversion.

The Church's Struggle

During the Advent season, we think of the darkness surrounding us, but also of the waiting. And there is the image of the candle illuminating the darkness, hoping and waiting for that day when we might be fully God's children, when we might live in harmony, with peace and justice. That image of Advent is the image I have of the Lutheran Church of El Salvador, and of all the churches who work with the poor in El Salvador. For almost 10 years the Episcopal, Baptist, Catholic, and Lutheran churches have worked closely together in serving the poor.

For many years these churches have been going through a time of darkness and persecution. They have shared fully in the crucifixion of the Salvadoran people. During the last 10 years 70,000 Salvadorans have been killed; 7000 have disappeared. Many of the victims were active members of Christian churches, especially of the Base Christian Communities (small Bible reflection groups of the poor).

Perhaps nowhere in Latin America, with the exception of Brazil, did the renewal of the church after the Second Vatican Council have such an impact at the grassroots level as it did in El Salvador. Progressive sectors of the Catholic church led the way in nourishing Base Christian Communities that were growing among the urban and rural poor during the early 1970s. The awakening of the poor that followed led into growing movements for social change. Trade unions, peasant cooperatives, and slum dwellers' organizations were all strengthened by the presence of church people.

The church became the leading prophetic voice by calling for an end to state violence against the poor. Archbishop Oscar Romero became a symbol for all the Americas of this church that took the side of the poor majority. And just as he paid for this commitment with his life, so have thousands of lay Christian leaders during the last 10 years. The blood of American church workers was mingled with the Salvadorans' when four American churchwomen were murdered in December 1980.

The violence against the churches has increased greatly since the end of 1989. There was a tremendous retaliation on the part of the Salvadoran government and military in the wake of the rebel offensive in November of 1989.

Six Jesuit priests, their housekeeper, and her daughter were brutally murdered by soldiers of the Salvadoran military. Medardo Gómez went into exile in Guatemala after receiving many death threats. There was a warrant out for his arrest by the authorities. Thirteen missionaries working with the Lutheran church were forced to leave either by threat or deportation. Baptist minister Edgar Palacios also had to leave the country temporarily. He is the head of the Permanent Committee of the National Debate for Peace, and has been instrumental in organizing many vigils and marches for peace. Father Luis Serrano, the head of the Episcopal Church of El Salvador, was detained and beaten along with many other of his church workers. One Catholic parish was mortared while hundreds of refugees crowded its facilities; many other churches were ransacked and desecrated.

An Advent gospel lesson helps us understand what the work of the Lutheran Church of El Salvador, and of the ecumenical church there, is all about.

> When John heard in prison what the Messiah was doing, he sent word by his disciples and said to him, "Are you the one who is to come, or are we to wait for another?" And Jesus answered them, "Go and tell John what you hear and see: the blind receive their sight, the lame walk, the lepers are cleansed, the deaf hear, the dead are raised, and the poor have good news

brought to them. And blessed is anyone who takes no offense at me." (Matt. 11:2-6)

When people in our churches in El Salvador—poor people who never really believed the gospel was for them, never believed they were truly children of God, never believed that they had rights, that they were truly human beings—hear the gospel preached, especially with such strength as we hear it preached by Bishop Gómez, it's as if the blind see and the deaf hear. Their lives are transformed. The lame walk, and lepers are made clean.

The gospel message for our church in El Salvador is much more than just words; it's actions. It's seeing to it that the lame walk, that the lepers are made clean. A major part of our work is health work. Not just Band-Aid solutions, but training people in their communities to help prevent problems that cause the majority of deaths in our country, like dysentery, or simple things like measles. Part of our work includes bringing medicines where there are no medicines, and teaching people how to help themselves live healthier lives.

The dead are brought back to life. I have seen how the Lutheran church is bringing back to life communities that were dead—dead spiritually or because the people were afraid.

I think of the people of El Paisnal, where about 15 years ago there were thriving Roman Catholic Base Christian Communities under the leadership of Father Rutilio Grande and a large pastoral team. A friend of mine, Sister Carmen, worked with that team. Their ministry was evangelical and empowering. The communities came alive with the gospel.

But on March 12, 1977, Rutilio was killed by members of the Salvadoran security forces. Hundreds of people including dozens of lay catechists in that area were killed in the subsequent army sweeps. The people were afraid—they either left, were killed, or stopped practicing their faith in an open way.

In 1982, the army killed 40 people in the eastern village of Candelaria. Many victims were members of the local Lutheran church. Chema, one of the survivors, fled to San Salvador with his family. He is functionally illiterate, but Chema's skills for ministry were recognized by Bishop Gómez. He was asked to go to the town of Aguilares as a lay evangelist and start a new ministry. To his surprise, Chema soon discovered that most of the people in Aguilares were originally from the surrounding villages, including El Paisnal. Before long the people asked Chema if the Lutheran church would accompany them back to their villages. Chema said yes. He and his family went out with the people the long 10 miles back to El Paisnal. Now this church community is being born again with the same people who used to be in the communities.

In March of 1989 I went to El Paisnal with Sister Carmen for the inauguration of the new Lutheran church, Buenas Nuevas (*Good News*) Lutheran Church—Carmen had not been to this area for more than five years; it was too dangerous for her. It was beautiful to see how happy Carmen was that those Christian communities she had left behind many years ago are thriving once again under the Lutheran church. She said to me, "Bill, this is the same church, the same church of Christ, whether it's Lutheran, Catholic, Baptist—what's important is that the good news is being preached to the poor."

Medardo Gómez is a pastor of this new church that is being born, but so are Carmen and Chema. During the Communion service Carmen was asked to serve the wine to the people, in clear recognition of her priesthood among these people.

The church in El Salvador believes that the gospel really is good news to the poor. Jim Wallis, the editor of *Sojourners*, a Christian magazine from Washington, D.C., recently wrote an article called "The Second Reformation." He said that what is going on in countries like El Salvador, and in places throughout the world where the church is growing much faster than it is here (for example in Africa and Latin America), is that a second reformation is happening. The first reformation centered around that wonderful truth—something Lutherans hold especially dear—that salvation is by faith alone. The church was dead, and that word of grace, that salvation is by faith alone, brought the church alive, brought the first reformation.

But now a second reformation is happening, especially in places like El Salvador. And what is that gospel insight? It is the simple truth that the gospel is good news to the poor.

What this is basically saying is that the gospel is to be preached to all. The majority of Salvadorans are either blind or deaf—I say this figuratively—or lame, sick, or in need of being brought back to life. As Father Jon Sobrino (one of the surviving Jesuit priests in El Salvador) has said, "To be poor in El Salvador is to be always close to death."

The full gospel that is preached in the Lutheran Church of El Salvador says that the gospel is good news to the poor. It means that the blind can see, the deaf can hear, the lame can walk, the dead are brought back to life. This does not deny that faith is the most important thing. These are people with a faith that astounds me at times, a faith in spite of the most tremendous repression and odds against them. They are simply saying that the message really is good news, that the church can be a message of salvation that transforms everything: a new heaven and a new earth.

The gospel lesson ends by saying, "Blessed is anyone who takes no offense at me" (Matt. 11:6).

Unfortunately many people are taking offense at what the Lutheran church is preaching in El Salvador, and they have for many years. Bishop Gómez was detained and tortured in 1983. Many of our church workers have been killed. One pastor was killed in 1984. Many have had to flee the country. Many have been threatened. Our church was bombed twice during 1989.

The miracle is that the church has grown in spite of all these problems. The Evangelical Lutheran Church in America recently published a world map of our global mission presence. At the bottom of the map it says that the Lutheran Church of El Salvador is one of the fastest growing Lutheran churches in the world.

I remember Bishop Gómez saying that when he was first detained and tortured, and finally let go after three days (he believes he was released because of all the pressure from the churches in the U.S. and Europe), he thought that when he returned to his church the next Sunday no one would be there to hear him preach. They would be afraid that being Lutheran would be considered subversive because the church had been preaching and acting in a way that was in favor of the poor. As Bishop Gómez has said, it's considered illegal to be a good samaritan in El Salvador, to preach the good news.

What happened in late 1989 and early 1990 is a systematic attempt to destroy the work of the churches in El Salvador, not just the Lutheran church, but all the churches that are working with the poor. How do they do this? How do they justify the killing, the detentions, the threats? Bishop Gómez has frequently said that the justification used is to say that what we are doing is communist, is subversive, and if you say that about another person, you can then kill them. Gómez says in very strong terms that this is blasphemy, because it's a way of saying that another person is not a human being, that we can do anything we want with that person.

That is what happened in November of 1989, 2000 people killed, mostly civilians. We've seen many people having to flee their homes. The leadership of the church is in exile.

But the church continues its ministry in El Salvador. The church does not depend only on its leaders or missionaries. The church is continuing its work with the people, led by the lay catechists and pastors. It is continuing to preach the good news throughout the country, and continuing to be for life, even in this time of darkness and death.

The Christians in El Salvador are speaking a word of prophecy to us in this time of hope by saying, "We are your brothers and sisters. You must hear our voices. We are like a candle—a very dim flicker right now—but we are a small light showing the reality of what's happening in our world. We illuminate injustice, but we are also a light of hope, of hope that we can be made right with God."

The message coming from El Salvador today condemns injustice, but also offers hope for all. This world can be a better place to live. There can be peace on earth.

We are not being persecuted in El Salvador just because we are Christians. Mere words don't get you into trouble there. Actions do. We are persecuted when we follow Christ, when we preach good news to the poor, when the blind receive their sight and the lame walk; when lepers are cleansed and the deaf hear, and when the dead are raised up. When that starts to happen, Christians are in trouble.

When I think of the church in El Salvador, especially the poor, I do not first think of the suffering. The joy of these Christian communities is what has impacted me the most. They know how to celebrate, to sing, to laugh—all of this along with the grieving, the sorrow.

I will end with some words Father Jon Sobrino spoke at an interfaith prayer service in San Francisco on December 1, 1989. Six of his colleagues had been killed in San Salvador just two weeks before.

Wherever there is love—real love—there is hope for the survivors. If we accept that amid the tragedy and sin of El Salvador, there are many, many people who have a great love, this is a message of salvation for us. It is good news. It helps us to keep on going. It means the resurrection is happening.

—*William Dexheimer*
February 1990

Chronology of Events in El Salvador

1821 Independence from Spain.

1879–82 Expropriation of communal indigenous lands by wealthy Salvadoran families, turning the lands into coffee, sugar, and cotton farms for export. These families of the oligarchy became known as the "Fourteen Families."

1932 An indigenous peasant uprising led by Farabundo Martí is turned back by the Salvadoran army under the command of General Maximiliano Hernández Martínez. Twenty to thirty thousand peasants are massacred in what became known as *La Matanza* (The Killing). Martínez ushered in 50 years of direct military rule in El Salvador.

1952 Rev. Robert Gussick (Lutheran Church–Missouri Synod missionary) arrives in El Salvador. Founding of the first Lutheran congregation in El Salvador.

1962 Rev. Ciro Mejía becomes first Salvadoran Lutheran pastor.

1963 Emergence of Christian Democratic Party in El Salvador.

1964–65   Consolidation of ORDEN (Democratic Nationalist Organization). ORDEN was founded by General José Alberto Medrano and Major Roberto D'Aubuisson. It was primarily a rural paramilitary network coordinated with the armed forces intelligence network. The so-called death squads originated with ORDEN.

1968   Meeting of CELAM (Latin American Episcopal Conference) in Medellín, Colombia. The Latin American Catholic bishops made a strong pastoral option for working with the poor majority. This decision was put into practice in El Salvador and throughout Latin America in the next decade—most notably with the birth of the BCC (Base Christian Community) movement.

1969–70   First BCCs in El Salvador (Zacamil-Mejicanos in San Salvador; Suchitoto, Chalatenango, San Vicente, and Morazán in the countryside).

1970–72   Direct repression against Catholic clergy begins. Salvadoran priest José Alas beaten, drugged, and raped by members of the National Guard.

1971   Formation of first guerrilla groups. The first guerrillas came from two different sectors of the Salvadoran left:

(1) former members of the Salvadoran Communist Party (PCS) who were disenchanted with the party's participation in the electoral process, and (2) radical students and workers from the Christian Democratic movement and the organized Catholic sectors (Catholic Action, Young Catholic Workers, etc.).

1972 A coalition ticket (Christian Democrats, Communist Party, and Social Democrats) headed by José Napoleón Duarte and Guillermo Ungo wins the presidential elections. The elections are stolen by the army with massive fraud. Many are killed in subsequent protests against the military. Duarte goes into exile.

1974 Six peasant cooperative members, active in the Catholic BCCs, are murdered by members of the National Guard in the village of La Cayetana, San Vicente. This marked the beginning of large-scale repression against peasants active in farm workers' organizations.

1975–80 Consolidation of the "popular organizations" in El Salvador, a new political phenomenon consisting of large coalitions of peasants, workers, teachers, students, slum dwellers, etc. Many came from the BCCs. For the most part the popular organizations had given up on the possibility of change through the electoral process. Instead they concentrated on mobilizing large numbers from these sectors in order to pressure the government and the oligarchy to effect changes in salary levels, working conditions, etc. The tactics used included strikes, demonstrations, and marches.

1977   *February* 20   Election of General Romero (no relation to Oscar Romero) to the presidency, with reports of massive voting fraud.

February 22   Oscar Arnulfo Romero consecrated Archbishop of San Salvador. He was considered the choice of conservatives within the church.

February 27–28   Army troops fire upon a massive rally in the Plaza Libertad in opposition to the new government. At least 100 are killed.

March 12   Jesuit Father Rutilio Grande is killed by members of the Salvadoran security forces in El Paisnal. Archbishop Romero celebrates the funeral mass two days later with an overflowing crowd at the cathedral. In June, hundreds of peasants, many of them Catholic lay catechists, are killed by the army in the area of El Paisnal, in what the army called "Operation Rutilio." Rutilio is the first of 10 priests to be killed in the years 1977–80. A popular slogan of the death squads is "Be a Patriot—Kill a Priest."

1978   The formation of first groups of mothers and relatives of the disappeared, with Archbishop Romero's support.

1979   *January*   Second meeting of Latin American bishops (CELAM), in Puebla, Mexico. An attempt on the part of conservatives in the Catholic church to turn back the reforms of Medellín is defeated.

October   Military coup takes over Salvadoran government. This sets up a reformist civilian-military junta.

1980   *early January*   Majority of civilians on the government junta resign in protest of massive army brutality against the popular organizations.

January 22   More than 200,000 march in San Salvador to mark the recent unification of all the popular organizations. Many are killed when troops attack.

March 23   Archbishop Romero calls on the army and security forces to stop the repression.

March 24   Archbishop Romero is assassinated.

May 14   Salvadoran army kills 600 peasants who try to cross the Sumpul River into Honduras.

Summer   Formation of CONIP (National Coordinating Council of the Popular Church), made up of sectors of the progressive BCCs throughout the country.

November   Formation of (Farabundo Martí National Liberation Front) guerrilla coalition.

November 28   Five leaders of the civilian opposition coalition FDR (Democratic Revolutionary Front) are murdered.

December 2   Four U.S. churchwomen are raped and murdered by members of the National Guard.

1981   *January*   Major FMLN offensive results in their military and political control of most of the northern region of El Salvador. This marks the beginning of full-scale civil war.

1982   *January*   Over 1000 peasants massacred by the Atlacatl Battalion in Mozote, Morazán.

Spring   Opening of Fe y Esperanza (Faith and Hope) Lutheran refugee camp in Nejapa.

1983   *April*   Detention and torture of Lutheran pastor Medardo Gómez.

Fall   Detention and exile of many people working with the Lutheran Church of El Salvador.

1984   *April*   Election of Christian Democrat José Napoleón Duarte to the presidency.

July-August   Large-scale army massacres in Cabañas and Chalatenango. Many survivors taken to Lutheran refugee communities.

October   First government–FMLN dialog (La Palma).

November 21   Lutheran pastor David Fernández of San Miguel is murdered by soldiers of the Third Brigade.

1985   *May*   First church-sponsored repopulation of people returning to the countryside from a Catholic refugee camp, in the village of Tres Ceibas.

1986   *January*   Beginning of "Operation Phoenix" in the area of Guazapa (30 miles from San Salvador). This was the largest military counterinsurgency operation to date. Thousands of refugees come into San Salvador. The newly opened Catholic refuge of Calle Real takes in many of these refugees.

January   Formation of UNTS (National Unity of Salvadoran Workers) culminates two years of slow resurgence of the popular organizations.

June   Luz Yaneth Alfaro, former member of the Nongovernmental Human Rights Commission, publicly accuses many popular organizations, including the churches, of being "fronts for the FMLN."

August 6   Medardo Gómez consecrated bishop of Salvadoran Lutheran Synod at Fe y Esperanza refugee camp.

October 10   Earthquake in San Salvador. The social service work of the churches is expanded significantly in the aftermath of the earthquake. The largest ecumenical church service in many years is held a few days after the earthquake.

November   National gathering of BCCs is held in San Salvador. Tension between the BCCs and Archbishop Rivera y Damas is at an all-time high. In early 1987 the Archdiocesan Department of Base Communities is dissolved.

1987   *January*   Repopulation of Lutheran refuge Fe y Esperanza to the village of Panchimilama.

August   Bombing of Fe y Esperanza Lutheran refugee camp (now primarily an orphanage).

September   Second government–FMLN dialog (San Salvador).

October 10   First massive repatriation of refugees from Honduras back to El Salvador. The churches work ecumenically in support of the returning refugees, greatly expanding their work in the countryside, especially in the conflict zones.

October 26   Herbert Anaya, President of the independent Human Rights Commission of El Salvador (CDHES), is assassinated by government death squads as he leaves home to drive his children to school.

1988   *July*   A "National Debate for Peace" is called together by the Archdiocese of San Salvador, to search for a peaceful solution to the conflict, involving as broad a representation of society as possible. More than 70 groups, including the Lutheran church, participate in the debate. Only groups not participating are from the far right. The conclusions of the debate support a negotiated solution to the conflict.

September   Formation of the Permanent Committee of the National Debate for Peace (CPDN), headed by Baptist minister Edgar Palacios.

November   First "March For Peace" sponsored by CPDN. Many Lutherans
participate.
December 28   Bombing of Resurrection Lutheran Church.

1989   *January*   FMLN proposal to take part in
elections under a number of conditions
including postponing elections until
September. The proposal becomes the
subject of debate at all levels of Salvadoran society, but it is ultimately
rejected by the ARENA (National Repub-
lican Alliance) party, which holds a
majority in the assembly.
February   Second "March For Peace."
March   ARENA party wins presidential
elections. Many accuse ARENA of being
tied to the death squads. ARENA was
formed by Roberto D'Aubuisson in 1980
after the dissolution of ORDEN.
April   Vice President elect Francisco
Merino accuses Father Daniel Sánchez, a
Spanish priest who pastors in the Mary,
Mother of the Poor parish, of being a
member of the guerrilla commando unit
that recently attacked his home. Archbishop Rivera publicly denounces the
accusation as being absurd; Merino does
not pursue the charge.
April   Death-squad style murder of
María Cristina Gómez, a woman active in

Emanuel Baptist Church and numerous women's organizations. The churches organize a "Chain of Hope" in memory of María Cristina, bringing delegations of women from North and South America and Europe to El Salvador.

June 2   ARENA takes power.

October 16   All-night "Vigil for Peace" at cathedral (sponsored by the CPDN) is marred by shooting by National Police officers infiltrated in the crowd. Three vigil participants are wounded.

October 20   Offices of the Lutheran church bombed the same night as homes of two prominent political opposition leaders are bombed.

October 31   Bombing of FENASTRAS (National Federation of Salvadoran Workers) trade union headquarters leaves 10 union members dead.

November 11   Beginning of FMLN offensive. Massive retaliation of Salvadoran military against neighborhoods and organizations suspected of sympathy with the FMLN follows. Many church leaders and missionaries are forced into exile, including Bishop Gómez and Baptist minister Edgar Palacios.

November 16   Six Jesuit priests, their housekeeper, and her daughter assassinated by soldiers.

1990   *January* 6   Bishop Medardo Gómez returns to El Salvador for two days to celebrate the Feast of the Epiphany at Resurrection Lutheran Church.

January 12   Assassination of Hector Oquelí in Guatemala. Oquelí was a prominent leader of the Salvadoran civilian opposition.

January 14   Massive repatriation to Morazán of Salvadoran refugees from Colomoncagua refugee camp in Honduras.

March 24   The 10th anniversary commemoration of martyrdom of Archbishop Oscar Romero, in San Salvador, and throughout the world.

Contributors

Mary M. Solberg is a Ph.D. student in systematic theology at Union Theological Seminary, New York, and is a free-lance editor, writer, and translator. From 1983 to 1986 she worked with (then) Pastor Medardo Gómez in El Salvador on behalf of the Lutheran World Federation. She has been actively involved with Central American issues since 1981.

William Dexheimer is a missionary pastor of the Evangelical Lutheran Church in America and has been working in cooperation with the Lutheran Church of El Salvador and the Roman Catholic Church for almost four years. He is also an associate missioner for the Disciples of Christ and the United Church of Christ. Pastor Dexheimer's ministry involves teaching and serving as an advisor for a pastoral training program with the Lutheran University and accompanying music in the Base Christian Communities. He is a frequent speaker, writer, and musical performer who often interprets the Salvadoran situation to North Americans and to church delegations visiting El Salvador. He left El Salvador in the fall of 1989 after receiving a death threat.

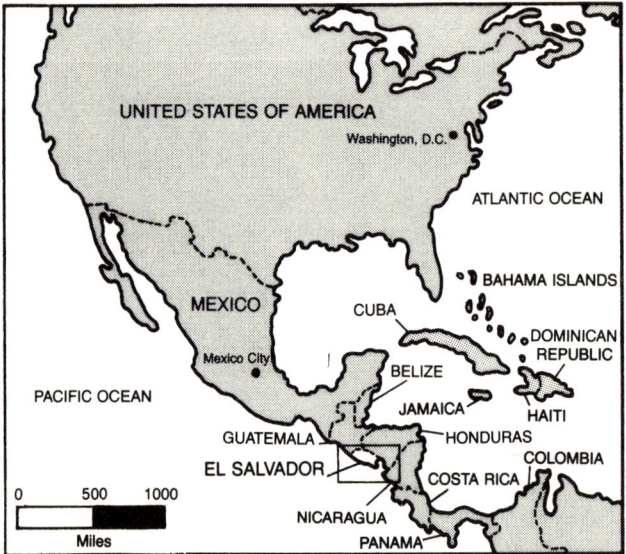

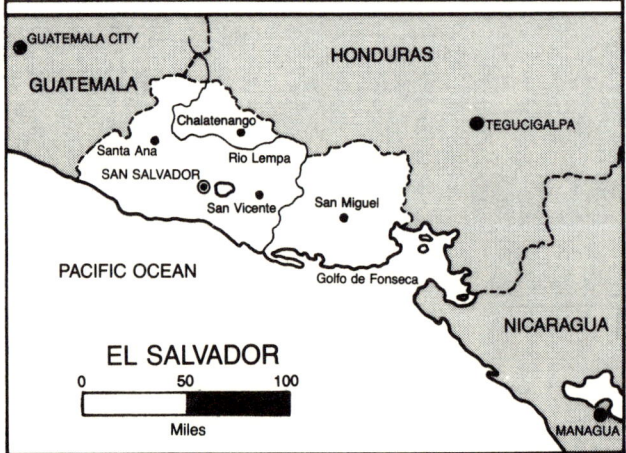

88

Map and Statistics

Area: 8,124 sq. mi. divided into 14 departments (smallest mainland nation in the western hemisphere)

Geography: Mountains separate country into three distinct regions: southern coastal belt, central valleys and plateaus; and northern mountains

Total population: 5,389,000

Density: 652 per square mile (the most densely populated in Central America)

Age distribution: 0-14 yrs., 45.2%; 15-59 yrs., 48.4%; 60 yrs. and above, 5.4%

Displaced: over one million (90% are children under 15 years of age)

Orphans: more than 9,000

Ethnic composition: Mestizos 92%; Indians 16%; Caucasians 2%

Language: Spanish (and among some Indians, Nahuatl)

Religion: Roman Catholic 81%; Protestant 18% (6,000–10,000 Lutherans)

Per-capita income: $470

Unemployment: urban 50%; rural 71%

Land distribution: 1% of farms comprise 71% of farmland; 41% of farms comprise 10% of farmland

Literacy rate: 65%

Life expectancy at birth: 58.8 years

Infant mortality: 86 per 1,000 live births (among total deaths of natural causes in rural areas, 47% are children under five who starve)

Physicians per 100,000: 27

Electrification: reaches 18% of total population

U.S. *aid* 1980-89: $3.4 billion

Sources: *El Salvador*: *A Country Guide*. Tom Barry. Albuquerque, N.M.: The Inter-Hemispheric Education Resource Center, 1990; *El Salvador*: *Central America in the New Cold War*, edited by Marvin E. Gettleman, Patrick Lacefield, Louis Menashe, David Mermelstein. New York: Grove Press, Inc., 1986; Children's Defense Fund; Non-governmental Human Rights Commission of El Salvador (CDHES); U.S. Aid Congressional Presentation

Suggested Resources

Books

Manlio Argueta. *One Day of Life.* New York: Random House, 1983. Fictional account of the realities of life for the poor in El Salvador.

Tom Barry. *El Salvador: A Country Guide.* Albuquerque, N.M.: The Resource Center, 1990. A complete background guide.

Phillip Berryman. *Liberation Theology: Essential Facts About the Revolutionary Movement in Latin America and Beyond.* Pantheon Books, 1987. An introductory explanation of the growth of the "popular church" movement.

Robert McAfee Brown. *Unexpected News: Reading the Bible with Third World Eyes.* Philadelphia: The Westminster Press, 1984. Challenges readers to understand Scripture from the perspective of the oppressed.

Pablo Galdámez. *The Faith of a People.* Maryknoll, N.Y.: Orbis, 1986. Describes life in a Salvadoran base community.

Penny Lernoux. *Cry of the People: The Struggle for Human Rights in Latin America—the Catholic Church in Conflict with U.S. Policy.* New York: Penguin, 1982. Focuses on the awakening of the traditional conservative Catholic Church to human rights abuses and the resulting conflict with the foreign policy of the U.S.

Oscar Romero. *The Violence of Love: The Pastoral Wisdom of Oscar Romero.* Compiled by James R. Brockman,

S.J. San Francisco: Harper & Row, 1988. A selection from the Bishop's own homilies and writings.

Jon Sobrino, S.J. *Archbishop Romero: Memories and Reflections*. Maryknoll, N.Y.: Orbis, 1990. As one of the Bishop's theological confidantes, Sobrino provides personal testimony and reflections on the Archbishop's impact on the development of his own theology and gives insight into Romero's personal struggle in living out his prophetic role.

Mary Solberg, ed. *Pregúntenos: A Resource Guide on Central America*. Chicago: Evangelical Lutheran Church in America, 1990. A listing of resources that reflect the perspective of the people of Central America intended for members of the ELCA.

Scott Wright, ed. *El Salvador: A Spring Whose Waters Never Run Dry*. Washington, D.C.: EPICA, CRISPAZ AND IRTFCA, 1990. Offers fifty reflections by Christians who have participated in base communities.

Newsletters and Reports

A Churchwide Blueprint for Action on Central America and Caribbean Concerns. Evangelical Lutheran Church in America. Adopted in Fall 1989 by the ELCA Church Council.

The Jesuit Murders: A Report on the Testimony of a Witness. Published 12/15/89. Lawyer's Committee for Human Rights, 330 - 7th Ave., Flr. N, New York, NY 10001.

KAIROS: *Central America: A Challenge to the Churches of the World*. A document signed by more than 100

Central American church leaders. 1988. Available from the New York CIRCUS, P.O. Box 37, Times Square Station, New York, NY 10108.

Letter to the Churches, P.O. Box 351, San Antonio, TX 78291. A translation of *Carta a Las Iglesias*, a publication of the Archbishop Oscar A. Romero Pastoral Institute of the University of Central America in San Salvador connecting Salvadoran communities to one another, and to the worldwide church.

Religion Report. Central America Resource Center, 1407 Cleveland Ave. N., St. Paul, MN 55108. Regular updates on news affecting the faith community.

Videos

La Lucha (The Struggle). New York: National Council of Churches, 1989. Examines the role of the church in El Salvador featuring interviews with Bishop Gómez, Jon Sobrino, U.S. Fr. Jim Barnett, and Ignacio Martin-Baro.

Once I Was Blind: A Pastoral Visit to Central America. Chicago: Evangelical Lutheran Church in America 1988. Follows Bishop Herbert Chilstrom on his journey to El Salvador, featuring an interview with Bishop Gómez.

Romero. New York: Paulist Press, 1989. A feature-length film depicting the Archbishop's conversion from a passive member of the traditional Catholic Church, to his role as prophetic martyr.

They Speak of Hope: The Lutheran Church in El Salvador. New York: Lutheran World Ministries, 1985. Provides an understanding of the persecution that results when the Lutheran Church in El Salvador carries out its ministry.